2/2/99

A New True Book

TORNADOES

By Arlene Erlbach

Acknowledgments
Mr. Paul Hoban, Meteorologist

Dr. David Changnon, Department of Geography, Meteorology Program,
Northern Illinois University, Dekalb, Illinois

CHILDRENS PRESS®
CHICAGO

PHOTO CREDITS

AP/Wide World Photos–38 (2 photos)

The Bettmann Archive–31

© Cameramann International, Ltd.–35, 37 (top left)

H. Armstrong Roberts–39; © E. R. Degginger, 23

PhotoEdit–© Myrleen Ferguson, 14; © Mark C. Burnett, 37 (right)

Photri–2, 6, 41, 43 (top left and right)

Root Resources–© Larry Schaefer, 9

© Scott T. Smith–13, 19

Tom Stack & Associates–© Tom Stack, 4 (top right)

SuperStock International, Inc.–© Harold M. Lambert, Cover; © Timothy White, 43 (bottom left)

Tony Stone Images–© U.S. Weather Bureau, 11; © Laurence Migdale, 37 (bottom left)

Travel Stock–© Buddy Mays, 15

Unicorn Stock Photos–© Martha McBride, 4 (bottom); © Betts Anderson, 20; © Eric R. Berndt, 45

UPI/Bettmann–7, 25 (2 photos), 26, 29, 32, 40, 46

Valan–© Phil Norton, 4 (top left); © Wouterloot-Gregoire, 17

COVER: Tornado

The funnel-shaped cloud
of a tornado

Project Editor: Fran Dyra
Design: Margrit Fiddle

*Dedicated to Margie and Laina,
who experienced a tornado.*

Library of Congress Cataloging-in-Publication Data

Erlbach, Arlene.
  Tornadoes / by Arlene Erlbach.
    p.   cm.–(A New true book)
  Includes index.
  ISBN 0-516-01071-9
  1.   Tornadoes–Juvenile literature.   [1.   Tornadoes.]
I.   Title.
QC955.2.E75   1994
551.55 .3–dc20   94-10472
                                                                CIP
                                                                AC

TABLE OF CONTENTS

Winds can be gentle breezes blowing through your window (top left). Stronger winds (top right) can shake the treetops. And sometimes winds are so strong that they knock over trees (bottom).

A VERY VIOLENT WINDSTORM

Winds help make our weather. They bring warm air. They bring cool air. Winds can be so slow and gentle that they hardly rustle the leaves. And winds can be so fast and strong that they knock trees over.

Sometimes, a funnel of rotating wind hits the ground. The funnel spins

A funnel cloud touches the ground in Minnesota.

at speeds of over 100 miles (160 kilometers) per hour. We call this funnel cloud a tornado.

Tornadoes are powerful windstorms. They have the

swiftest and most destructive winds on earth. Sometimes people call tornadoes "cyclones" or "twisters" because the winds spiral and twist.

A tornado's strong winds can rip roofs off buildings. They can smash houses

This rare photograph shows a tornado tearing the roof off a building in Fresno, California.

and uproot large trees. Sometimes they pick up people and carry them for hundreds of yards.

Tornadoes have overturned railroad cars and picked up entire herds of cows. Fortunately, tornadoes usually last only a few minutes and cover just a few miles.

Tornadoes occur all over the world, but most tornadoes strike the midwestern United States. Almost one thousand

Tornado damage at Barneveld, Wisconsin

tornadoes hit the United States each year.

Most tornadoes happen in April, May, or June. During this "tornado season," about twenty to forty tornadoes touch the ground each week.

9

THUNDERSTORMS MAY CAUSE TORNADOES

Meteorologists are scientists who study weather. They do not know all the reasons why tornadoes occur. But they have learned that certain weather conditions make tornadoes likely.

Tornadoes dip down from the clouds of severe thunderstorms. To understand how tornadoes

A funnel-shaped tornado descends from the dark clouds of a thunderstorm.

develop, it helps to know how thunderstorms form.

In the spring, warm, moist air blows north from the Gulf of Mexico. Cool, dry air blows south from Canada.

The warm, moist air carries a great deal of water vapor. Water vapor

11

is water in the form of a gas.
The gas is made up of
billions of tiny bits of water
called water molecules.

When the cool air and
warm air meet, the cooler
air slides underneath the
warm air. The warm air
that rises into the sky is
lighter than the cool air.

As the warm air moves
upward, it cools and
condenses, or changes
into drops of water. This
happens when the water
vapor's molecules join

Fluffy cumulus clouds are formed by masses of water droplets.

together and form water droplets. The droplets drift high into the sky. They become clouds.

Clouds are enormous masses of water droplets. At first the clouds are white, fluffy cumulus

13

clouds. Then they collect more water and grow big and dark. These clouds are called cumulonimbus clouds. Cumulonimbus clouds are over 6 miles (9.6 kilometers) tall and

Dark cumulonimbus clouds produce thunderstorms.

A heavy thunderstorm with lightning in northern New Mexico

more than 1 mile (1.6 kilometers) wide. They produce thunderstorms.

Thunderstorms bring heavy rain, thunder, lightning, wind, and sometimes hail. During a thunderstorm, there are

15

columns of wind rising and coming down from the clouds.

The rising columns of air are called updrafts. They feed more warm air into the storm. The descending columns are downdrafts. They bring raindrops and cooler air to the ground.

A typical thunderstorm lasts from forty minutes to an hour. It stops when all the rain has come down from the clouds. The downdrafts have cooled the ground and there are

Huge cumulonimbus clouds can make the daytime almost as dark as night during heavy rainstorms.

no more warm updrafts to feed the storm.

Most thunderstorms do not produce tornadoes. Only severe and supercell thunderstorms make tornadoes likely.

17

SEVERE AND SUPERCELL THUNDERSTORMS

Severe thunderstorms are very powerful. Their winds move at speeds of 58 miles (93 kilometers) per hour or more. They can produce heavy rain and hail at least ¾ inch (2 centimeters) in diameter.

Some severe thunderstorms cover an area of over 100 square miles (250 square kilometers). These are called supercell thunderstorms.

Supercells consist of enormous cumulonimbus clouds.

The rain from a supercell thunderstorm can last for more than three hours. Supercells often produce strong winds and unusually large hail.

After a hailstorm, pieces of ice called hailstones cover the ground. They will soon melt in the warm air.

Hail is formed when strong updrafts during a thunderstorm pull the falling rain high up into a thundercloud, where it is very cold. The rain freezes and becomes hail.

Sometimes hail does not

fall all the way to the ground. Strong updrafts inside the cloud may bring the hail up again. The hail collects more moisture. On each trip, the hail grows larger and heavier. Hail may rise and fall within the cloud many times before it is heavy enough to fall to the ground.

Thunderstorms have other types of air movement besides updrafts and downdrafts. High above the ground, cool winds are moving. They usually move east. Close to the ground, warmer winds blow slowly. They usually move north.

In a severe or supercell thunderstorm, these winds blowing from different directions above and beneath the storm may cause an updraft to spin. The updraft then becomes a funnel of rotating air called a mesocyclone. And a mesocyclone may become a tornado.

A tornado moves through a Wisconsin suburb.

FROM MESOCYCLONE TO TORNADO

The mesocyclone may suck up more warm air. This makes it spin faster. Then it stretches down from the clouds as a funnel cloud. A funnel

23

cloud becomes a tornado when it hits the ground.

About 1,700 mesocyclones develop from thunderstorms in the United States each year. Some mesocyclones spin for a few moments and then disappear. But about half of all mesocyclones become tornadoes.

Mesocyclones from large supercell thunderstorms may drop more than one funnel-shaped column of wind. So some tornadoes

Killer tornadoes struck in Laurel, Mississippi, in 1987 (left) and in Huntsville, Alabama, in 1989 (right). The damage was immense and many lives were lost.

have one large tornado with smaller tornadoes revolving around it. These are the fiercest tornadoes. They smash everything in their paths and often kill people. Fortunately, most tornadoes are not that deadly. **25**

A tornado touches down just south of Salina, Kansas, in 1973.

WHAT HAPPENS DURING A TORNADO?

Tornadoes usually strike a few minutes after a thunderstorm has stopped. Often, hail has just fallen. The atmosphere is calm. It seems that the bad weather is over. But the worst is yet to come.

A loud rumbling sound roars through the air. It sounds like a freight train. That is the sound of a tornado.

Usually, rain and hail do not fall during a tornado, but rain may come down on rare occasions.

Tornadoes are very unpredictable. A tornado might touch the ground once and then disappear.

Or it might rise into the sky again and travel farther. Then it dips down and strikes the ground miles away.

Some tornadoes move in a straight path. Others hop along the ground in loops or move in a zigzag pattern.

The funnel-shaped tornado cloud moves along the ground at about 20 to 50 miles (32 to 80 kilometers) per hour. The whirling winds inside the tornado can spin at more

A tornado roared through Wood River, Illinois, in 1949, turning this house upside down.

than 200 miles (320 kilometers) per hour. These winds cause the most destruction.

The tornado's strong winds act like a giant vacuum cleaner. They suck up houses, trees, people, and cars.

A tornado's color comes from the materials whirling inside it—whatever it has picked up. Sometimes a tornado picks things up and drops them gently. For example, a jar of pickles picked up by a tornado was found miles away in a ditch—unbroken.

Tornadoes have sucked up all the fish and frogs from a pond and carried them away. When the tornado dropped them,

Tornado damage in the city of St. Louis, Missouri, in 1896

people thought it was
raining fish and frogs.

Tornadoes have ripped
blankets from people. They
have even pulled the
feathers off chickens.

Most tornadoes last only a
few minutes, but some

A room in a school in Murphysboro, Illinois, where sixty children were caught by a tornado in 1925

tornadoes last for hours and travel through more than one state. In 1925, a tornado covered 295 miles (475 kilometers). It lasted three and one-half hours, causing death and destruction in Missouri, Illinois, and Indiana.

HOW STRONG ARE TORNADOES?

Tornadoes are classified by their wind speed. Scientists use the Fujita-Pearson Tornado Intensity Scale to measure tornadoes. The rating system is named for the people who designed the scale–Dr. T. Theodore Fujita, a tornado researcher, and Allen Pearson of the National Weather Service.

The Fujita-Pearson scale rates tornadoes from F0 to

THE FUJITA-PEARSON TORNADO INTENSITY SCALE

Classification	Windspeed	Damage
F0	40-72 mph (64-116 kph)	Light
F1	73-112 mph (117-180 kph)	Moderate
F2	113-157 mph (181-253 kph)	Considerable
F3	158-206 mph (254-331 kph)	Severe
F4	207-260 mph (332-418 kph)	Devastating
F5	261 mph + (419 kph +)	Incredible

F5. Only about 3 percent of tornadoes are rated F4 and F5. These tornadoes develop from supercell thunderstorms. They cause total devastation and often kill people.

Most tornadoes are rated F0 or F1. They develop from less severe

Dr. T. Theodore Fujita is the world's leading authority on tornadoes.

thunderstorms. Their wind
speed is under 112 miles
(180 kilometers) per hour.
But these tornadoes are
dangerous too. They
topple chimneys, blow
down power lines, and
push cars off the road.

PREDICTING TORNADOES

Meteorologists at the National Severe Storms Forecast Center in Kansas City, Missouri, watch for tornadoes constantly. They study satellite pictures of weather conditions. They receive information about the weather from radar and weather balloons.

Over 300 weather stations in the United States watch for thunderstorms that

Meteorologists at the National Weather Service (left) study information received from measuring instruments. At right, a weather balloon is released. It will rise high in the sky, where its instruments will gather information about the wind and weather.

produce tornadoes. They make sure that radio and TV stations know when to warn people.

Amateur photographers took these pictures of tornadoes in the 1940s.

Volunteers are also trained to be tornado spotters. If they spot a funnel-shaped cloud, they notify the weather bureau. Then the weather bureau warns people in the area.

Waterspouts look like tornadoes, but they are usually smaller and their winds are not as strong.

WATERSPOUTS AND HURRICANES

Waterspouts are tornadoes that occur over water. The rotating wind picks up the water and swirls it around.

Waterspouts last longer than tornadoes that hit land. But the winds are

39

This view, shot from space, shows the huge, whirling cloud mass of a hurricane.

gentler and they do not spin as fast.

Hurricanes are enormous masses of whirling thunderclouds that form over the ocean. They can last for many days and cover hundreds of miles.

Sometimes clouds break away from a hurricane and cause severe thunderstorms. These violent thunderstorms can create the funnel-shaped clouds that cause tornadoes.

TORNADO SAFETY

It is important to understand what the terms *tornado watch* and *tornado warning* mean. During a tornado *watch,* conditions are right for a tornado. A tornado may occur within the next few hours.

Make sure you have emergency supplies such as food and water. Put away anything outside that can be blown around. Bring pets indoors. Stay tuned

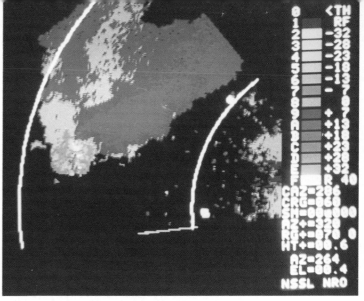

Many people who live in areas where tornadoes are frequent have storm shelters to protect them (left). Radar pictures (right) help meteorologists track tornadoes.

to your radio or TV for further information.

During a tornado *warning,* a tornado has been seen by someone or shown up on radar. Seek shelter at once.

Go to a storm cellar or

43

the southwest corner of your basement. If you have no basement or storm cellar, lie flat under a table or in a stairwell. Stay away from windows. Tornado winds can shatter them and send glass flying.

If you are outdoors, lie down flat in a low place, like a ditch. If you are in a car with adults, warn them not to try to outrace the tornado. Leave the car. Move to the lowest spot possible. Lie flat and cover your head.

Nothing can be done to stop the terrible damage that tornadoes leave in their wake, but improved warning systems can save many lives.

Today, meteorologists are better able to predict tornadoes. And timely warnings help people protect themselves. Tornadoes still cause great property damage. But even in the most violent storms, few lives are lost.

WORST TORNADOES IN THE U.S.

Year	Place	Deaths and Injuries
1840	Natchez, Mississippi	Over 370 dead
1896	St. Louis, Missouri	Over 300 dead
1924	Lake Erie area	99 dead
1925	Missouri, Illinois, Indiana	695 killed; 3,000 injured
1936	Mississippi, Georgia. Two days of tornadoes	Over 600 dead
1965	Six states from Iowa to Ohio	271 dead; 5,000 injured
1974	Five states from Alabama to Ohio. 148 tornadoes	350 dead
1985	Ohio Valley and Canada. 41 tornadoes	90 dead; over 1,000 injured
1990	Seven states from Wisconsin to Kansas. 50 tornadoes in four hours	13 dead
1991	Kansas, Texas, Oklahoma, Arkansas, Missouri, Nebraska, Iowa. More than 70 tornadoes in one day	About 30 deaths
1994	Tornadoes in Alabama, Mississippi, Georgia, North Carolina, and South Carolina	Over 40 deaths

WORDS YOU SHOULD KNOW

atmosphere (AT • muss • feer)–the gases surrounding the earth; the air

cloud (KLOWD)–a mass of water droplets floating high in the air

condense (kun • DENSS)–to change from a gas to a liquid

cumulonimbus cloud (kyoo • myoo • loh • NIM • bus KLOWD)–a large, dark cloud that gives rise to a thunderstorm

cyclone (SY • klone)–a mass of whirling wind; a tornado

downdraft (DOWN • draft)–a strong downward wind current inside a storm cell

gas (GAS)–a substance that is neither solid nor liquid and that has the same form as air

liquid (LIK • kwid)–a substance that flows more or less freely and may be poured from a container

mesocylone (MEH • so • SY • klone)–whirling winds inside a storm cell

meteorologist (me • tee • or • RAHL • uh • jist)–a scientist who studies weather

molecule (MAHL • ih • kyool)–the smallest particle of a substance that can exist and still keep its chemical form

predict (prih • DIKT)–to say what will happen in the future

radar (RAY • dar)–a device that finds objects by bouncing radio waves off them

rotate (ROH • tait)–to go around in a circle; to revolve

satellite (SAT • ih • lite)–an artificial body that revolves around the earth high above the surface and contains instruments that measure conditions on the earth

spiral (SPY • ril)–to follow a path that moves in a circular motion

updraft (UP • draft)–a strong upward wind current inside a storm cell

Opposite page: Tornado destruction in Gainesville, Georgia, in 1936

water vapor (WAW • ter VAY • per)–water that has been turned into a gas by heating

weather balloon (WETH • er bah • LOON)–a balloon that carries instruments high in the sky to measure weather conditions

INDEX

About the Author

Arlene Erlbach has written more than a dozen books for young people in many genres including fiction and nonfiction.

She has a master's degree in special education. In addition to being an author of children's books, she is a learning disabilities teacher at Gray School in Chicago, Illinois. Arlene loves to encourage children to write and is in charge of her school's Young Author's program.